An Interview With

A Black Lawyer Fighting for Justice

By

ZULU ALI, ESQ.

Introduction by Rosa Nunez-Kobi

DEDICATION

Dedicated to the Loving Memory of My Grandparents, A.D.
and Bessie Reynolds

ABOUT THE AUTHOR

Zulu Ali is a practicing trial attorney, businessman, social commentator, and activist. A former police officer and U.S. Marine Corps veteran, he earned a doctorate in law (J.D.) from Trinity International University; a masters in administration of Justice (M.S.) and business (M.B.A.) from University of Phoenix; and an undergraduate degree with a focus on African Studies from Regents College through a consortium with Tennessee State University.

He is a postgraduate scholar of international law and treaty law at Euclid University, West Africa and a doctoral scholar of business with a research focus on Pan-African business and trade at California Southern University.

Attorney Ali is the founder and principal attorney at the Law Offices of Zulu Ali and Associates, LLP based in Riverside, California , where he focuses on representing persons accused of crimes, immigrants, and persons seeking civil justice in state and federal courts. Ali is also admitted to represent persons at the African Court of Justice and Human Rights in Tanzania and the International Criminal Court at The Hague, Netherlands.

Attorney Ali and his law firm take on extremely difficult cases and matters that provide an opportunity to make changes in the law, through the courts, when the law is unjust. Attorney Ali served as Director of the American Committee for United Nations Oversight, an advocacy group that lobbied the United Nations for police reform in 2015. He is the Director of the Stop and Frisk Academy, which mentors and trains at-risk youth to deal with police encounters; Director of the Southern California Veterans Legal Clinic, a legal clinic offering no-cost and low-cost legal services to military veterans; and a member of the National Conference of Black Lawyers.

In 2020, Attorney Ali was inducted as a biographee in the Marquis Who's Who in America for excellence in law and activism. In 2017, Attorney Ali was recognized as one of the most influential African American Leaders in Los Angeles by the National Action Network founded by Reverend Al Sharpton. Attorney Ali has been Honored as a Top Lawyer by the National Black Lawyers-Top 100 and National Trial Lawyers-Top 100; a Top 10 Lawyer by the American Academy of Trial Attorneys, American Institute of Legal Counsel, American Jurist Institute, and Attorney & Practice Magazine; Litigator of the Year by the American Institute of Trial Lawyers; and Rue Ratings Best Lawyer in America.

He is the founder and CEO of 10 Nubian Queens & 5 Kings Media, a mass media production company focusing on black family and social justice content in film, radio, theater, music, and book publishing. Ali produced the documentary film Purpose & Freedom: Keep Your Hand on the Plow, which premiered at the Wilshire Screening Room in Beverly Hills in 2017 and on-demand (PurposeandFreedomMovie.com); wrote and produced the stage play Purpose & Freedom: The Story of Attorney Zulu Ali & Aracely Morales, which premiered at the Hudson Theater in Hollywood in January 2020; and wrote and produced a musical compilation with various artists titled The Discography of Zulu Ali. Attorney Ali authored the books *Lecture on Black America and American Justice: A History & Paradigm of Retributive Psychosis* (2016); *When the Jury, Money, Votes, and Pride Comes Black* (2020); and *Black Man's Religion: Islam or Christianity* (1997), a copy of which is in the Collection of Rosa Parks Papers at the Library of Congress.

Additionally, Zulu Ali is the host of the nationally syndicated radio talk show Justice Watch with Attorney Zulu Ali which broadcasts from an NBC Radio studio in Redlands, California; and he is a member of the National Black Radio Hall of Fame (Chicago chapter).

Ali has been married to his wife (Charito) since 1986, has four adult children (Christine, Whitney, Ashley, and Lynda), three grandchildren (Amayah, Tye, and Izem), and resides in Southern California with his family. Born and raised in central Tennessee by a single mother, Linda Reese Harvey, who Ali considers his hero; he is the grandson of the late A.D. and Bessie Reynolds; Perry and Catherine Reese; and Mr. and Ms. Edward Castleman.

As a youth, Ali attended Tennessee public schools, where he participated and lettered in varsity football. He is a descendant of Africans of Ibo and Balante distinction brought to central Tennessee in the eighteenth century and subjected to forced subjugation. His family has resided in the central Tennessee area since the eighteenth century and, in spite of forced subjugation, has contributed significantly to national wealth, community service, military service, and a variety of professional areas.

CONTENTS

INTRODUCTION

By Rosa Nunez-Kobi, Executive Producer, Justice Watch Radio

For over four centuries, the vicious cycle of systematic racism has deeply entrenched the oppression of African Americans as a necessary component of the American system. The history of racial injustice in the United States has contributed to a discriminative and painful legacy. A historic legacy that offers a complete system of constitutional protections to Caucasian suspects, and denies those very same rights to minority defendants. The narrative of racial difference has made the price of fighting for justice a costly one. As a result, those refusing to be officers of the court are constantly subject to judicial scrutiny.

In order to uncover the racial disparity that pervades the U.S. criminal justice system, we sit down to have a conversation with our very own host attorney Zulu Ali. Through this special edition of Justice Watch Radio, we examine institutionalized racism, a dynamic which further exacerbates the oppression of African Americans within the judicial system. Most notably, in this discussion attorney Zulu Ali reflects on his experience from humble beginnings to becoming an award winning trial-lawyer. As an African American lawyer fighting for justice, attorney Zulu Ali identifies the distinct practices within our criminal justice system. Practices which work hand in hand with other institutions to further deepen the systematic oppression of African Americans.

Furthermore, attorney Zulu Ali uncovers the prejudiced nature within the judiciary branch. He expands on the implicit judicial bias which directly influences the mass incarceration of African Americans in the United States. This intellectual conversation is equally a call for the American population to adopt a more selfless mindset. As a man of integrity devoted to his faith, Zulu Ali links the lack of unity in or communities to the broken value system in America. In sum, attorney Zulu Ali actively educates the reader on higher level social justice concepts. However, by expanding on his lived experiences as an African American lawyer, attorney Zulu Ali urges the reader to think critically about structural racism within our criminal justice system.

INTERVIEW

[Rosa Kobi-Nunez interviews Attorney Zulu Ali]

Interviewer:

Thank you for tuning into this special edition of Justice Watch. I am here with our very own host, Attorney Zulu Ali. We are here to talk about the cost and consequences of fighting for justice. When you talk about race and how different kinds of groups have been trying to fight to be included in this constitution and be included in this country as a black lawyer, what are the conflicts that you've faced trying to really fight for justice and be there for your clients, and also trying to be an officer of the court.

ATTY ZULU ALI:

I mean, it's really, really difficult because what you're doing is that you have a system of justice in America that has systematically oppressed black people. And the system, basically as an officer of the court, then in many ways you stand to be somewhat of an instrument that assists in some way of that oppression, right?

I mean, it doesn't make any difference what position that you have, like for example, the

President of the United States. And let's just say during the

Obama administration, you had a black man that was the President of the

United States. And even though you had a black man that was a President of the United States, you continue to have the same type of discrimination.

And some may argue you had more discrimination, an oppression that was going against people of color during his administration because it's a system.

Interviewer: Of course.

ATTY ZULU ALI: It's almost like a machine, right? Let's say you build a machine that makes wrenches, and then you decide that now we want to make screwdrivers, you use the same machine. It's still going to produce wrenches-

Interviewer: Yeah, of course.

ATTY ZULU ALI: regardless. And that's kind of what happens when you're talking about a court system that has... It's the routine that African-Americans are not given the same type of justice as other individuals. That's the way the system works. And just because you have an individual that's put into that system, doesn't mean that that individual is going to change the output, right?

Interviewer: That makes perfect sense.

ATTY ZULU ALI: And so, whether you're talking about black judges, for example, we know there was a situation with a judge that basically brought to light the whole idea that a prosecutor was systematically excluding black jurors, and actually ended up getting suspended for six months because of that. I think it's Olu Stevens, Judge Stevens. He was an African-American.

Because what was wrong with that? Because as a judge, you're not supposed to do that [even if it is right and just].

Interviewer: Yeah.

ATTY ZULU ALI: Because that interferes with the system of justice. And as a result of that, he was suspended for six months for doing that. And so, I think that when you're talking about as a black man who is in a situation, who really wants to change things and challenge things, then you're going to have issues with the system, because the system isn't made that way.

Interviewer: Yeah.

ATTY ZULU ALI: So, it's a very difficult situation to be in because you're going to be subject to constant judicial scrutiny and sanctions. Because if you choose to make a difference in the lives of people, a real difference, then you're going to have a problem-

Interviewer: Of course.

ATTY ZULU ALI: ... right? There's no way of avoiding it because the system is made a particular way. And when you begin to start challenging that or saying,

"You know what? I'm going to file a motion. I'm going to bring to light the fact that there happens to be a predominantly or almost all white jury. And my defendant happens to be African-American or Mexican-American.

And he deserves a jury of his peers."

Interviewer: Yeah.

ATTY ZULU ALI: And if you bring that to their attention, then there could be some pushback, right? They may not like that. So, what if the judge says, "You know what?" Doesn't agree with you. Then are you supposed to just shut up and allow it to happen? Or if you become vocal and be an advocate for your client.?

So, there's a thin line between being a zealous advocate and being disrespectful to the court.

Interviewer: Wow.

ATTY ZULU ALI: Right? That's a very subjective idea. If the judge denies your motion, you're saying, "I want to strike this jury because it doesn't look like my client. And I don't believe he's going to get a fair trial because it doesn't represent a cross section of the community." And then the judge denies it and you continue to argue the issue. Then, you're not supposed to be there.

Bring me somebody that's going to allow this system to continue to do what it normally does. And that is to be unfair and unjust to black and brown people, which is the way... That's part of our system.

Interviewer: Yeah.

ATTY ZULU ALI: Right.

Interviewer: Yeah. And it makes perfect sense that you say, that if you're being an officer of the court, they're trying to make you to cater to the needs of the system, but as a person of color, you're really trying to fight for justice for your clients.

ATTY ZULU ALI: Right.

Interviewer: And in doing so, you explain how you run into this thin line of crossing the line over to protect your client or being that officer of the court. And I guess my question is, what is your purpose and what really kind of inspires you to fight for justice in such a system?

ATTY ZULU ALI: For me personally, I believe that we all have a purpose.

Interviewer: Yes.

ATTY ZULU ALI: We did a documentary called Purpose and Freedom, and it was really about an experience that I had because it is frustrating. It is frustrating realizing that the system is not going to allow you to make changes, unless you're willing to get bumps, bruises, scratches, and death, potentially death. That's the nature of the game. And sometimes you ask yourself, once you go down that road, why are you doing this?

And I remember that I had this dream and in this dream, in this particular case that I was dealing with after one of my clients was ridiculed and completely disrespected by a judge in her case, I had a dream and I was just really fed up with it. And honestly, I felt like I was done.

Interviewer: Wow.

ATTY ZULU ALI: Never quit because I don't think I'll ever quit, but I just felt like I was done. And I remember in this dream, I saw myself in this cemetery in

Lynchburg, Tennessee. And I was at the gravestone of my grandfather and my grandmother. I could see them. They were standing there. And my grandfather was sitting there. He was very stoic. He wasn't saying anything. And my grandmother was there and I was talking to her about,

"What am I doing this for it?"

I remember that she began to... The song that she used to sing to me, it was a Mahalia Jackson song. It was called Hold On. Her version of it was Glory is Coming, keep your eye on the prize, glory is coming. And she says, "It's not your glory, it's their glory." So, I began to understand that basically, sometimes your purpose is not necessarily your prize, but sometimes it's other people's prize.

And I've never had a situation where I went through this process where somebody did not benefit from it. And so, in other words, there's other individuals that are benefiting from what I have to go through and what

I'm doing, and it kind of rejuvenated me and kind of made me realize that that was really my purpose. My purpose was to come into this world and to touch other people.

Interviewer: Wow. It's truly inspiring to hear that you feel like your purpose, it's in a way, something bigger than yourself. And yeah, that's truly amazing and inspiring to hear because I feel like you don't really hear that often.

ATTY ZULU ALI: Right.

Interviewer: You really hear the small talk kind of response of, "I'm a lawyer because of the money." Or, "I'm a lawyer because I just want to have that kind of character and be known as that." But it's truly inspiring to hear that you're working for something bigger than yourself.

ATTY ZULU ALI: Right.

Interviewer: And to know that you're willing to take the punches for your clients.

You're willing to take that hit because you know it's something greater. It's going to be something greater in the end.

ATTORNEY ZULU A...: Right.

Interviewer: And I feel like we've talked a little bit about race and how that comes into play with the system and how it's really in charge of really oppressing individuals in a way. And I wanted to ask, why do you think the system in itself has been formulated in such a way to continue oppressing a certain group of people?

ATTY ZULU ALI: Right. I mean, I think that it is fear. I mean, again, it's not fear of like physical fear. I don't think they fear that the person is going to do anything to them. I don't really believe that. I think it could be the byproduct in some circumstances as to why people feel that way, but I think it's a bigger fear as to who you can become. Humanity never ceases to disappoint me.

For me personally, I was always raised from the perspective that everyone is trying to get the... When you're trying to do good or be good, then that's really what we live for. But the reality of it is, is that we live in a very selfish world.

Interviewer: Absolutely.

ATTY ZULU ALI: And I think that people basically fall into five basic types of categories.

One are people who are inspired or moved by comfort. All they want to do is just be comfortable. The second group of individuals are people... I call them that are moved by acceptance. All they want to do... And we see those people. They are have inferiority complexes and they just want to be accepted.

The third are the type of individuals that want recognition and prestige, right? And we know those individuals. Prestige is good, recognition. They just want attention, period, even if it's bad. We see that on reality shows, right?

Interviewer: Yes, definitely.

ATTY ZULU ALI: Then the fourth group of people are what I call achievers. People who are looking for personal financial access. They're obsessed with achievement, right? And then the last is the impact and people who come into this world and they want to make an impact. They're far and few between. They're the Charles Hamilton Houston's, they're the Malcolm X's, they're the Dr.

Martin Luther King Jr's, they're the third good Marshall's, Avon Williams.

These are these people I call impact players.

85% of the people in the world fall into the first three categories, either comfort, acceptance, or recognition or prestige. 10% are achievers. And then the fifth are impact players, right? And impact players are people who come to this world who are moved by impact, are kind of at the top of the food chain, but are far and few between, and are moved by something that typically they can't really explain.

Interviewer: Yeah.

ATTY ZULU ALI: You know what I mean? And they're the 5% of the people that are truly satisfying. For me, for example, there's this level of satisfaction. On one hand, you feel like you're a tortured soul, right? Because once you enter the arena of truly trying to make a difference in this world, then ultimately you realize that you've committed yourself to something and you're satisfied knowing that whether it's today, tomorrow or 50 years from now, if you leave this world and you're in your final resting place, you've done your duty, right?

Interviewer: Yeah.

ATTY ZULU ALI: There's a sense of sadness because you understand the world.

Interviewer: Yeah.

ATTY ZULU ALI: I think it's a gift that some people have that they understand that.

Interviewer: Yeah.

ATTY ZULU ALI: But the thing about everybody else is that everybody is chasing something, that they'll never be ultimately fulfilled because they're chasing something.

And even when they get it... I mean, we see those people like the achievers. I mean, we have people, the... How many billionaires do we know that committed suicide or millionaires that committed suicide?

I mean, these people are never happy regardless of what you give them, but just to circle around to what you're saying, as far as why people are the way that they are, as far as the system and people being racist, and again, it's just a matter of inferiority and they're fearful of who you will become.

Interviewer: I see.

ATTY ZULU ALI: Right? I mean, you do have people on the low level of the food chain that believe those sorts of things. But in the final analysis, I think subconsciously, there's the fear that what would happen if these individuals were actually put into a position of power?

Interviewer: Yeah.

ATTY ZULU ALI: Historically, if society flips, then will these people do to us what we did to them? Right? That's really what it boils down to. It's just a whole thing of you don't let your foot off of someone's neck if they're going to get up and they're going to kill you. You keep your foot on their neck. So, I think that basically when you do so much dirt to people and you treat people so badly, the fear is that if I allow things to be fair and not be happy with their oppression and my perceived entitlement, then I would lose it.

Interviewer: I see.

ATTY ZULU ALI: See, people aren't moved by fairness.

Interviewer: Yes.

ATTY ZULU ALI: You know what I mean? The only time that people are concerned about fairness is when they're treated unfairly.

Interviewer: Of course.

ATTY ZULU ALI: Do you see people marching for fairness when they are treated special? I mean, very seldom does that happen? You know what I mean? So, the only time that people March against police brutality is when they can identify with police brutality.

Interviewer: Of course.

ATTY ZULU ALI: When people march against the way that the justice system is treating people in just, whether it's courts or whatever is, they're touched by it insome way. You know what I mean?

Interviewer: Mm-hmm (affirmative).

ATTY ZULU ALI: So, you don't see people striking with union workers unless their family and friends of people in the union. And that's just unfortunate that we do not have people who care anything about justice except for themselves.

And the reason why we have such a bad society and that humanity is in a condition that it's in is because we are selfish people.

Interviewer: Yes.

ATTY ZULU ALI: It's just outright selfishness. I was talking last week about the upcoming presidential elections on the show that we just did. And I was talking about the fact that there's all kinds of buzz. I listened to all kinds of talk shows about the election, but not one conversation about who is a good person. You know what I'm saying? Who is going-

Interviewer: Very true.

ATTY ZULU ALI: Who is going to treat the lowest man on the totem pole as good as the highest man on a totem pole.

We're talking about strategy. We're talking about why is it that we're more interested in the fact that someone went to

Yale than we are about someone who basically fought his country.

Interviewer: Yeah. Wow.

ATTY ZULU ALI: You know what I mean?

Interviewer: Yeah.

ATTY ZULU ALI: I mean, it's just like the President of the United States, people were not outraged about what he said about John McCain. He says that just because he had an issue with John McCain, he never gave him any kind of credit for the fact that he says, "My heroes don't get captured." I mean, just think about that. And we're cool with that.

But at the same time, we're mad at Colin Kaepernick for taking a knee.

Interviewer: Of course.

ATTY ZULU ALI: So, that kind of tells you exactly what to... And he's critical of Colin

Kaepernick for taking a knee.

Interviewer: Yes, definitely.

ATTY ZULU ALI: Right? So, you're going to be mad at this man for taking a knee protesting against police brutality, but you're going to be disrespectful to a man who spent years in a POW camp get who went through all kinds of torture. So,

I think that when you began to start understanding who we are, the hardest thing to do is to look at yourself and we don't look at ourselves as individuals. And so, what happens is that basically, if you're able to look beyond that selfishness and you're able to go out in the world and you begin to start fighting for people, even when those individuals don't even appreciate the fact that you're fighting for them, whether they do or not.

And not to mention the haters because the haters come out of the woodwork, then you have to deal with the repercussions of not being well, the 95% of the people who go through their day, not doing anything for nobody else, except themselves. It's the same thing with our politics.

Interviewer: Yeah. Of course. It's interesting that you mentioned most people are in that 95% and throughout, you mentioned different, important figures of individuals who have purpose and have been attacked. And we have seen this throughout history with different civil rights advocates like Martin

Luther King, Malcolm X, and people of color have been specifically targeted because of their purpose as a public servant and as an activist, because you're not only an attorney, but you're also someone who's out there in the community and very involved.

ATTY ZULU ALI: Well, I think ultimately, my purpose is to touch as many people as I possibly can and make the biggest impact that I possibly can to, in somehow, some way help make this world a better place than it was when

I got here. I remember when I was a little kid, my grandmother used to have this saying, and I used to ask her, "Grandmama, what are you doing?" And she used to always reply. She used to say, "I'm writing my obituary. What are you going to say about me when I'm gone?" And I remember that one of my favorite Mark Twain quotes was, he says, "The two most important days in a man's life is when he's born and when he knows why he's born."

And I felt like that when I remember when my grandmother passed, I went to her funeral, actually, I'd seen her the day before. And I remember this one particular day earlier when she had made that statement to me when I was a kid. And when she would say, "What are you all going to say about me when I'm gone?" She would smile. She had a certain type of smile.

And I remember when she passed away and the day before she was actually in the hospital, and I remember we were talking, she seemed fine.

And when I left the hospital, she smiled at me. And it seemed like from my mind, it was the same smile when she would say, "What are you going to say about me?" Right? So, when she passed away and we went to the graveyard and I could kind of feel that-

Interviewer: Wow.

ATTY ZULU ALI: ... right? And the way I felt when she left this world and because she was an extremely giving person like she would give you everything that she had if you needed it, right? And the way she made me feel, and then the day when she passed away, the way she made me feel and I always said that, "That's what I want." I want to live my life in a way in which when

I'm in my final resting place, that my children, my wife, and my family, and my friends feel the same way I felt on that day. And I always say, "I thank my grandmother for giving me the second most important day of my life." And that's what I feel like my purpose is, is from that moment on my entire life changed.

Interviewer: Wow.

ATTY ZULU ALI: I mean, the things that I chose to do in life, it was a pivotal point in my life, that particular experience being there thinking of how I felt on that that day at the graveyard. You see what I mean?

Interviewer: Yeah.

ATTY ZULU ALI: So, it was her legacy that changed my life and made me realize that's really what I want to do because other than my grandfather, that's the closest person who had passed away to me, right? And so, her legacy made me realize what life is all about because I never really thought much about death, but at that moment, at that time, I felt like I knew what my purpose was.

And I don't think I was ever fearful of death from that moment on.

Interviewer: Wow.

ATTY ZULU ALI: You know what I mean? I felt that I needed to get on this mad dash to make a difference. And that's my legacy. I mean, that's my purpose.

What's going to be my legacy? Is it going to be selfishness? And as you know, the great comedian Paul Mooney used to say, "You've never seen a

Brinks truck following a Hertz." Because you can't take any of those things with you. And even when you leave money, most people squander it or fight over it.

But when you leave goodness, and you change people's lives, then you leave something that's lasting and that's going to benefit you in this world.

And it's going to benefit you in the next world. And that's really how I'm moved. I wish I could give some sort of secular prolific reason why I want to do that. But in the following analysis, that's really what I want to do.

That's what life is really all about.

Interviewer: Yeah. Wow. And it's interesting how it all ties in because you talk about this purpose that's greater than yourself and how that in itself inspired you from your grandparents. And you can see your own purpose and you leaving your legacy with everything that you do in that community. You have to stop and frisk Academy where you talk to youth about police encounters and all of that. You touch on that youth community, you talk on the radio to implore people about social justice issues that are prominent in their communities. You try to bring this jury reform initiative to light, to really expose the flaws within the justice system. It's interesting how it all ties into that bigger purpose where you might not know it, but you are actively kind of doing this, expanding a greater purpose through everything that you do on your daily life. And that's amazing.

And I'm sure that as a lawyer, you definitely see other lawyers who kind of have that sense of purpose as you do, but I'm sure you also see other lawyers who really don't.

ATTY ZULU ALI: Yeah. Yeah. I mean, it's kind of interesting in the profession and just quickly, the way that I'm specifically making my choice to go to law, become a lawyer. My grandfather, his name, A.D. Reynolds, who as a little boy, I spent a lot of time watching him. I grew up in a single parent household. So, my mother worked two jobs and my grandfather was a janitor. And at night, he would clean law offices. And there's one attorney, he cleaned his law office. His name was Tyrus Cobb. And when I was a kid, maybe seven or eight years old, he took me in the law library. He introduced me to Attorney Cobb and he said, "This is my grandson. And he's going to be the next Avon Williams."

Interviewer: Oh, wow.

ATTY ZULU ALI: And that's when the Attorney Cobb started telling me about Avon

24

Williams and all these great lawyers who changed the world. And so, I left there thinking, "That's what I wanted to do."

Interviewer: Of course.

ATTY ZULU ALI: Right? And then of course, after my grandfather passed away, when I was... he passed away when I was in the military. And later on, after that, I went to court to chance to record regarding the name change petition that I had filed. And when I walked in front of him, he was actually the presiding judge. He went from being Tyruss Cobb-

Interviewer: Wow.

ATTY ZULU ALI: ... to being the judge. And he said, "Ladies and gentlemen, I want you to meet the next Avon Williams." And he started telling me about how great of a man my grandfather was. And I became extremely emotional and left.

And went to Tennessee state and Rhode and embarked on this journey to become a lawyer. But the type of lawyers being from the South, lawyers were seeing differently than they are today.

When I was growing up, lawyers were people like Avon Williams, Z.

Alexander Looby, Thurgood Marshall, all these great men who were trying to change the world, right? And it wasn't the money because money was not really... They were not known to be wealthy men. They were just known to be men who were willing to fight and stand up for people who could not stand up for themselves.

And that's what I was raised to understand a lawyer to be. And Charles

Hamilton Houston, who was the Dean of Howard University Law School and the mentor to many great civil rights lawyers, one being Thurgood

Marshall, who paired at the same statement that as a black lawyer, you're either a social parasite or you're a social engine.

Interviewer: Wow.

ATTY ZULU ALI: And I believe that either you can be a lawyer and do nothing except suck the life out of everything. It's just like now... I mean, I was watching a game show where they said what professions are known to be liars. And they said, lawyer was number one, right?

Interviewer: Wow.

ATTY ZULU ALI: And so, the idea of being a lawyer now is I don't know if it's different. I think there's more of a social parasite than the social engineer. And I believe that every lawyer who has the opportunity every day to actually touch other people and make a difference, some people don't feel like that's their obligation or their duty.

Interviewer: Yeah.

ATTY ZULU ALI: I mean, I just think that's where the profession went. And you have to ask yourself this question, there's a lot of Hispanic attorneys. There's a lot of

African-American attorneys. There's a lot of attorneys of different walks of life. But considering that many of what goes on in the justice system hasn't changed, how can so many people come from these communities and go out there and get involved and you do not see a more expansive change? And it's because again, if you're not willing to put it on the line, it doesn't really matter.

If you are a Hispanic judge and you are the son of immigrants or the daughter of immigrants, and you become an immigration judge, what are you going to do to change things for people who are being mistreated or an immigration system that seems to be unjust, what are you going to do?

If you're going to sit on the bench and just be a face with a name that sounds Hispanic, and everybody gives you awards and pats you on the back, then you really haven't done anything.

Interviewer: Yeah.

ATTY ZULU ALI: If you're African-American who basically have come from the inner cities and understand what it's like in many different cases, whether it's the inner city or anywhere else, and you sit up there and you have a robe and you get these awards, and everybody says, "He's a black judge," but you don't see any changes, what does it matter? It doesn't matter. It doesn't mean anything because the system is the problem.

Interviewer: Of course.

ATTY ZULU ALI: And if you go along with the system and you don't do anything to make a change, then it's the same old thing. That's the reason why it takes more than just being a face. You can't just get into the system and just do your job if you're not making a change as a prosecutor. You know that they're mistreating people, you know that their judicial discretion is not really good as far as determining who's going to be prosecuted or the type of sentence that's going out. What are you going to do?

If you're going to get up every day, get your paycheck and be a face, it's really not going to matter. The same thing with being police officers.

There's been African-American police officers who have been involved in corruption, who've been involved in abusing individuals and are present when it happens. But if you're not going to do something from within the system to make a change, then it doesn't really matter.

So, that's where I say that, basically just if you're going to do it, they're going to come after you.

Interviewer: Yeah.

ATTY ZULU ALI: You know what I mean? And if you're not ready for that, then you're not going to make a change that nobody goes... I mean, if you're not doing anything, it's just like the legislators. Like some of those legislators right now who are getting a lot of backlash, are they getting just recognition or are they really making a change? Right?

Interviewer: Yeah.

ATTY ZULU ALI: Whether you're talking about what do they call them now? The big four, right? Or whatever they call them. That's part of it. I mean, what's going to happen? There's consequences. There's cost. Unless you're just going to go to your box and just do what you're supposed to, then whatever. I mean, it's just like Clarence Thomas is a Supreme Court Judge.

Interviewer: Yeah.

ATTY ZULU ALI: Now, is there anything that he's done in that position has changed the lives of people of color?

Interviewer: When we talk about cost and consequences of attorneys, and public officials, what are the specific kind of repercussions that an attorney or a public defender or anyone in the justice system can face for going outside the law or using the law for that?

ATTY ZULU ALI: Yeah. Well, I think that, especially those who are actually employed like a public defender or a prosecutor then the issue is employment. I mean, obviously they can put pressure on your employer to terminate you. You could lose your job if you're not playing ball, because I mean, the whole idea about human beings is that at my age, the one thing that I've realized is that everybody makes mistakes and sometimes mistakes sometimes can be very subjective. That's why they call it the Practice of Law. Because basically, people kind of think about the law as being this really black and white situation where this is wrong. The law says this, the law... that's how most people see it.

But the thing about the law is that it's extremely ambiguous. That's why when you look at court decisions, Supreme Court decisions, and they always talk about what type of decision? Was it five, four? Was it six, three? Was it seven, two? Because you have to ask yourself this question.

If there's an issue of law, in fact presented to nine individuals and the ruling is not equal, you have a dissenting opinion who completely disagree with everybody else and you have the majority opinion. So, that teaches you, what is the law? Who was to say that the dissenting opinion is better than the majority? You see what I mean?

Interviewer: Yeah.

ATTY ZULU ALI: And the reason why that's the law. So, what if you file something or pursue something that is seen by the justices as the minority view, right?

Then as an attorney, someone can say, "You made the wrong decision, that wasn't the right decision." Everything that you do because the law uses words like reasonable, right, intentional. And obviously, you can't go inside someone's mind to make a determination as to what's reasonable or intentional. Or when we talk about the issue of due process or when we talk about the issue of juries, right?

I'm of the opinion that if you have an individual who happens to be

African-American and the entire jury pool is white, you got a problem with whether that is a fair jury, but I think I'm right, right? I think that I'm right about that, but you have someone else and apparently just about everyone else that hasn't flown. You can't say because there's no white people on the jury that this black man can not get a fair and impartial jury.

There's people who believe that. And so, when you talk about the issue of consequences, then it goes back to the whole idea that as an attorney and you're practicing law and you're fighting for certain things, your decisions, everything is a risk because every time you pursue something, you're going to lose. Somebody is going to lose. And if you lose like Johnnie

Cochran lost Geronimo Pratt's trial. Of course, 20 years later, he won the appeal. But does that make him a bad lawyer? You know what I mean? Or let's just say his aggressive manner in which to try to get that appeal or get that conviction overturned, could that be seen as someone who is doing something frivolous? You see what I mean?

Interviewer: Yeah.

ATTY ZULU ALI: Everything in the law is open for scrutiny in a way based upon how you see it.

Interviewer: Yes.

ATTY ZULU ALI: You could do something that you think in your mind is okay, and could be completely against the law.

Interviewer: Yeah.

ATTY ZULU ALI: So the point is, it's easy to fall into a trap, even when you're doing things the way you're supposed to and even within the system. Once they want to come after you, then they can come after you. And oftentimes, it could be something as simple as saying, "Your Honor..." Like, for example, the way that Barry Scheck talked to Judge Ito in O. J. Simpson case. Someone could say, "I don't like the way you're talking to me, I'm going to sanction you."

Interviewer: Wow.

ATTY ZULU ALI: "I think that you're being disrespectful." Or you may have someone who pursues an action based upon their interpretation of the law and the courts could sanction that person.

Interviewer: Wow.

ATTY ZULU ALI: Or any of those things. The filings that you do or mistakes that you... I mean, it's just one of those things that are like, even in some of these immigration cases where someone is seeking asylum. There has been people who were found to have... like I say, you filed a frivolous claim because he's from Peru and nobody from Peru is scared to go back to Peru.

Interviewer: Wow.

ATTY ZULU ALI: Nobody's scared to go. It's so vast. And one person ruling can make that difference. Like, for example, with Brown v. Board of Education, the mere filing of Brown v. Board of Education could have been seen as frivolous, right? Let's think about Dred Scott, where the United States Supreme court said that you could not file a lawsuit because an African-American is not a human being. The Supreme Court said that.

So, anytime that you filed a lawsuit on behalf of an African-American, after the ruling in Dred Scott could have been a frivolous.

Interviewer: Wow.

ATTY ZULU ALI: Right?

Interviewer: Yeah.

ATTY ZULU ALI: And he could have been sanctioned. He could have been suspended. You could have been disbarred because you're fighting for something that the court got wrong.

Interviewer: Wow.

ATTY ZULU ALI: Right?

Interviewer: Yeah.

ATTY ZULU ALI: So, that's the thing, is that if the courts get it right all the time, there's no need for lawyers, right? You don't need a law if the courts got it right. The only reason you need lawyers is because the courts get it wrong all the time.

Interviewer: Yeah.

ATTY ZULU ALI: Right? And so, if the courts are getting things wrong, then you got to say that the court's wrong, or you might have to tell the judge that he's making a bad decision. You know what I mean? It's almost like slavery was illegal. Not allowing black people to vote was legal. Jim Crow was legal.

All of these things that our country has done had been co-signed by the judicial branch, meaning that it was illegal.

And so, what are you supposed to then just imagine if we lived in a society where we accepted what the court said? Plessy versus Ferguson, that's the law of the land that meant separate but equal. Jim Crow was okay. You could do that. And so, if you don't challenge it, then you're up against something. And the only reason is the politics of the day.

Interviewer: Yeah.

ATTY ZULU ALI: You see what I mean? So in other words, there could have been time where someone would have said, "No, that's not a righteous claim. Your argument, we've already said that we've already said that, like for example, even the people fighting that want to overturn Roe v. Wade, is that frivolous?

I mean, I think that the court got it right. But the mere argument against it, and if the courts are always right, why are you fighting it?

Interviewer: Wow.

ATTY ZULU ALI: You see what I mean? So, that's what makes the law of this whole thing where it's about politics. So, if you're going against the grain and you have to go against the grain, because the courts get it wrong all the time.

Interviewer: Yeah.

ATTY ZULU ALI: And when you do that, that's what happens. I mean, if you're making this big splash, they have to get rid of you. Are they going to try to get rid of you or discourage you?

Interviewer: Yeah.

ATTY ZULU ALI: Do you want to be the bad guy that's able to go into courts and be able to argue things for people who are being mistreated? That's not what they want. They want you to be quiet and conform. So, if you're being quiet and you conform, then they don't have to worry about you. That means that they get to rule and do things the way that they want to. And then when you begin to start not being quiet, "I'm going to fight against it," they don't like that. I mean, who goes out fighting for things and nobody comes after them? You see what I mean?

Interviewer: Sure.

ATTY ZULU ALI: So, that's the thing. I mean, when you make noise, so most people go in and they tuck their tail and they bow their head, and they treat the... I mean, sometimes I've represented veterans that have got injured in war, right? And he's being judged. He is being scrutinized by a judge who never fought in a war, a prosecutor who's never fought in a war. Nobody in that courtroom has sacrificed more than the guy that's been accused of the crime.

Interviewer: Wow.

ATTY ZULU ALI: But yet and still, he has to give respect to the judge.

Interviewer: Wow.

ATTY ZULU ALI: Because he wears a robe, right?

Interviewer: Yeah.

ATTY ZULU ALI: That means if you go to an Ivy League School, you get a law degree, it doesn't matter whether you do court work, litigation work, but you know the right people. You're appointed to the bench and you wear a robe. That means that you have the right to make decisions over people's lives, no matter who you are. Now, you don't think that that's going to bump heads with somebody else.

I mean, that's typically how people get appointed. I mean, they run for office in some places, but oftentimes they get appointed as well. So that's another thing. Because I ran for office and I got appointed to this judgeship that, that gives me the right to... It's politics.

Interviewer: Yeah.

ATTY ZULU ALI: That's really what it is. So, you have the right to make these laws and determine fairness when the way you got into office. Does that mean that you're qualified to do that, to make those kinds of decisions over somebody's life? So, we don't question that. You see what I mean?

Interviewer: Yeah.

ATTY ZULU ALI: And there's consequences when you do and there's dire consequences. And that's the reason why our judicial system and our system is ineffective.

That's why so many innocent people are convicted for things that they didn't do. That's why the people are overcharged. That's why you see these prosecutors who are being caught hiding evidence. I've seen an interpreter in court the other day who was telling me a story about when they started and they happened and asked the prosecutor, "Do you think this guy's guilty?" And the response was, "Are you kidding me? This is Orange

County. It don't matter whether he's guilty or not. The jury is going to convict him regardless."

Interviewer: Oh, wow.

ATTY ZULU ALI: And so, you have people who are 25, 26, 27, 28 years old or older, given that type of power-

Interviewer: Wow.

ATTY ZULU ALI: ... over other individuals. And they don't care about humanity.

Interviewer: Yeah.

ATTY ZULU ALI: There's not a discussion about humanity. I've had situations where victims have come and said they lied and literally have prosecutors say, "Well, in light of the fact that the victim had actually... he's done something before,

I think I could still get a conviction." You see what I mean? So, that's what you're dealing with that. And when you're fighting to get something like that, you're going to make enemies and people are going to try to take you out.

Interviewer: Yeah. Wow. It's almost exasperating to hear that as a lawyer and as an attorney who is trying to fight for justice, you are still on the line of being unemployed or being sanctioned or being held to these unfair consequences by the courts because you're not being that officer that caters to the needs of that system.

ATTY ZULU ALI: Right.

Interviewer: And I guess my question is, as somebody who is really willing to take the consequences and what comes with fighting for justice, what is your advice? What is your hope for the future, especially with this current administration in this current political system?

ATTY ZULU ALI: Well, I mean, my hope is that people somehow some way become a little bit more... not a little bit more, but a whole lot less selfish.

Interviewer: Yeah.

ATTY ZULU ALI: I think that basically, we're entering a time period where... Sometimes I feel like our time is running out. And I feel like that basically we've become so complacent that we feel like that there's not going to be any consequences to all the dirt that we've done.

Interviewer: Yeah.

ATTY ZULU ALI: And we've been given ample opportunity to address the dirt that we've done. And ultimately, we can pay for that. You know what I mean? I mean, I truly believe that one day, somehow some way... it's not like we're the first nation that felt that we were powerful than everybody else. And history teaches us that every powerful superpower has ultimately lost their title.

Interviewer: Yes.

ATTY ZULU ALI: And I think that now we've been given chance after chance after chance to make amends for the things that we've done. And if we continue to avoid our opportunity to be a better nation and make up... I mean, look at it like this. We charge people and hold people to standards that we don't hold our own nation to.

We will not allow people to do things and make amends for things that we've done ourself. We talk about even prosecutors. That's how we feel like we can solve every problem is make a law and prosecute people.

We're always trying to prosecute people for making mistakes.

Interviewer: Yes.

ATTY ZULU ALI: But we don't look at ourselves as a nation. You see what I mean?

Interviewer: Yeah.

ATTY ZULU ALI: So, it's just like, how can you tell me that you have to pay for this, all these people, whether you're talking about children, sex trafficking or trafficking children. It amazes me because people are outraged with that type of a crime, but to think that that's how we became a nation, trafficking human beings, right?

Interviewer: Yeah.

ATTY ZULU ALI: But nobody looks at it that way or families that were split up, people that were raping women on these plantations who were probably children.

Crimes. Like crimes to humanity that could not be met by any other place.

But that is what it is, I believe in forgiveness and redemption.

Interviewer: Yeah.

ATTY ZULU ALI: And we are a nation that we're always talking about people taking responsibility for their actions. And I think until we begin to start taking responsibilities for our own actions, then I think that ultimately, it could be our undoing.

Interviewer: Yeah.

ATTY ZULU ALI: That's my fear. And I think that people aren't listening.

Interviewer: Yes.

ATTY ZULU ALI: We feel like, you know what? Nothing could ever go wrong. We have a strong military, we have a great economy, we're the strongest nation in the world. But we are oppressing people and still today separating children from their parents in 2019 and putting children in cages and mentally destroying and in some cases, physically destroying children and not one peep, not one thing. You don't hear a country outraged. That should be literally impossible in 2019. There's no way, I mean, when it comes to a child being separated from their parents at the... Sanction by the government should be something that you... and that kind of sets... If you want to know where we are as a society, you go to the border and you go to the prisons and you'll know what type of society that you're in.

You see what I mean?

Interviewer: Yeah.

ATTY ZULU ALI: And I think that until we began to start looking at ourselves and caring about other people other than ourselves, before it's too late, then I think that I believe that we're going to perish literally, that we will lose because that's the way the world works. And then we've been blessed by giving an opportunity to make amends and we didn't do it.

Interviewer: It's interesting that you mentioned that. We're at this point in history where it's kind of scary to think about everything that's going on and how people are still being oppressed. And with that in mind, how can the average person contribute to this change?

ATTY ZULU ALI: Yeah. Well, I think that we need to... and I keep going back to this whole idea of about not being selfish.

Interviewer: Yeah.

ATTY ZULU ALI: I think that the average individual has to begin to start trying to understand their fellow man. I mean, we're so quick to judge other people without really, truly trying to understand. Some of the people with some of the highest degrees at some of the most prestigious institutions tend to be some of the most ignorant people that we know just simply because they castigate and think certain things are a certain way.

I mean, they're very stereotypical and we throw people into certain groups and that's our form of training in our country. But I think that my advice is to stop being trained and focus on being educated, right? So, these institutions... The perfect word is when someone says that they've been trained at an Ivy League School. For example, I'm Harvard trained or I was trained at Berkeley. And training is a perfect thing, but I think that we have to begin to start thinking beyond these social, economic, political paradigms that we kind of box ourselves into.

And because we do that, we don't think for ourselves, right?

Interviewer: Mm-hmm (affirmative).

ATTY ZULU ALI: So it's just like, for example, when we think about the... And I hate to keep going back to our Commander in Chief, but let's just say we talk about the president and Trump and some of the things that he says, and that many of his followers are going to blindly do what he says or follow him regardless.

And I think that we have to begin to start... And you have to ask yourself this question too. Again, and I don't want to be so completely negative, but he tapped into a sentiment in this country that was brewing. He did not create it. He just recognized it, exploited it, and now he kind of motivate those individuals to come out and do some of the things that they would normally potentially would not do, because that is a degree of hatred for your fellow man.

Interviewer: Yeah.

ATTY ZULU ALI: And I think that when you have a degree of hatred for another human being, when you absolutely don't know anything about them based upon the color of their skin. And one of the things that I do want to be clear about is that it's not just white people, hatred and this whole thing. The question is, I mean, we see other individuals that come into this country from other places that harness that same type of sentiment even towards

African-Americans.

Interviewer: Yeah, yeah.

ATTY ZULU ALI: It's a human problem. But clearly in this country, it's driven by this whole idea of European supremacy. And basically, the European supremacy is a misnomer because it isn't because they're superior. It is a degree of inferiority, a significant degree of inferiority, why someone would mistreat another person that they deem in their head incapable of being able to do anything.

So, you would not have to go out of your way to oppress people unless you were fearful that they may rise. And I think that what happens is, is that there's a sense of entitlement that we have as human beings. In order for you to be entitled in the

United States, you have to, in some way, align yourself with that supremacy ideology.

Interviewer: Yeah.

ATTY ZULU ALI: Right? So in other words, when people come to the United States and supremacy is somewhat in their mind seen as a matter of entitlement, then when people relate to that particular group, then it's a more of an avoidance, they have to act this way because if I can identify with these people, then they will not look at me and see who I really am, if that makes any sense.

Interviewer: Yeah, yeah.

ATTY ZULU ALI: But I think until we begin to change the way we are as human beings and begin to start thinking more of our fellow human beings, not just for some prop for TV. We talk about it, but that's not who we are. You know what I mean?

Interviewer: Yeah.

ATTY ZULU ALI: And so, we just need to figure out ourselves and ways of making this world better by touching other people, figuring out if there's somebody else that I can touch, that I can feel. The one question is that as human beings, what makes us so judgemental and love the opportunity to disrespect and to do bad things to somebody else?

Then there's people that could see a wounded dog and feel worse than they could a wounded man in the street.

Interviewer: Sure.

ATTY ZULU ALI: That's the kind of society we live in. And the question is, is that just who we are? How do we get out of that? And in many ways, I really don't have the answer because if I could change hearts, then I would.

Interviewer: Yeah.

ATTY ZULU ALI: But I think that sometimes when you do good things for people, that sometimes it does change people's hearts. So, I think the more people who are willing to do good to other people, then maybe we can change one heart at a time, and maybe we can save our nation. We got homeless veterans, right?

Interviewer: Yeah.

ATTY ZULU ALI: So, a nation that loves its country, loves its freedom, and love the men and women who fight for it and we don't even take care of those people. So, I mean, that tells an entire story.

Interviewer: Yeah. With that in mind, we're getting ready to close. Thank you so much,

Mr. Ali for lending us your time. We look forward to having you tune into our Sunday broadcast. For further information, log into justicewatch radio.com. Thank you so much for tuning in.